NO TRUCE WITH THE FURIES

R.S. Thomas was born in 1913 in Cardiff and now lives in Gwynedd. He won the Heinemann Award in 1955, the Queen's Medal for Poetry in 1964, and the Cholmondeley Award in 1978, and has received the Welsh Arts Council's literature award three times. He has been nominated for the Nobel Prize for Literature for 1996.

He has published more than twenty books of poems since his first collection *The Stones of the Field* appeared in 1946, including *Selected Poems 1946-1968*, published by Bloodaxe, and its sequel *Later Poems 1972-1982* from Macmillan, publishers of his later collections *Experimenting with an Amen* (1986) and *The Echoes Return Slow* (1988). Seren Books have published two other collections, *Ingrowing Thoughts* (1985) and *Welsh Airs* (1987), as well as his *Selected Prose* (1983), Sandra Anstey's recently expanded *Critical Writings on R.S. Thomas* (1983) and J.P. Ward's study *The Poetry of R.S. Thomas* (1987).

His autobiography, *Neb*, written in Welsh, was published by Gwasg Gwynedd in 1985, and his *Collected Poems* by Dent in 1993. His most recent poetry collections are *Counterpoint* (1990), *Mass for Hard Times* (1992) and *No Truce with the Furies* (1995): all three are published by Bloodaxe, and each has been made a Poetry Book Society Recommendation.

R.S. THOMAS

No Truce with the Furies

BLOODAXE BOOKS

ISBN: 1 85224 360 0 hardback edition
       1 85224 361 9 paperback edition

First published 1995 by
Bloodaxe Books Ltd,
P.O. Box 1SN,
Newcastle upon Tyne NE99 1SN.

Bloodaxe Books Ltd acknowledges
the financial assistance of Northern Arts.

Cover printing by J. Thomson Colour Printers Ltd, Glasgow.

Printed in Great Britain by
Bell & Bain Limited, Glasgow, Scotland.

For Alice

Contents

Geriatric

What god is proud
        of this garden
of dead flowers, this underwater
        grotto of humanity,
where limbs wave in invisible
        currents, faces drooping
on dry stalks, voices clawing
        in a last desperate effort
to retain hold? Despite withered
        petals, I recognise
the species: Charcot, Ménière,
        Alzheimer. There are no gardeners
here, caretakers only
        of reason overgrown
by confusion. This body once,
        when it was in bud,
opened to love's kisses. These eyes,
        cloudy with rheum,
were clear pebbles that love's rivulet
        hurried over. Is this
the best Rabbi Ben Ezra
        promised? I come away
comforting myself, as I can,
        that there is another
garden, all dew and fragrance,
        and that these are the brambles
about it we are caught in,
        a sacrifice prepared
by a torn god to a love fiercer
        than we can understand.

Fathoms

Young I visited
this pool; asked my question,
passed on. In the middle years
visited it again. The question
had sunk down, hardly
a ripple. To be no longer
young, yet not to be old
is a calm without
equal. The water ticks on,
but time stands, fingerless.

Today, thirty years
later, on the margin
of eternity, dissolution,
nothing but the self
looking up at the self
looking down, with each
refusing to become
an object, so with the Dane's
help, from bottomless fathoms
I dredge up the truth.

Still Point

In the universe one
world beneath cloud
foliage. In that world
a town. In the town

a house with a child,
who is blind, staring
over the edge of the universe
into the depths of love.

Lunar

The moon never sets
in Northampton. Every time
I pass through it stares
at me from a window
of the asylum and is always
at the full. Don't be misled
by those likenesses of it
when it was new and shone
down on unenclosed meadows.
As it waxed it became
bald. It was a skull
where names chased one another
without end, wife and sweetheart
hurrying by like shadows
over the corn. For ignorance
time stops by a flower.
Young he was in his own
sky, rising at mornings
over unbrushed dew,
with no one to introduce
him to earth's bustling creatures
but his love. It was love
brought him, as it brings
all of us in the end, face
against glass, to demand
brokenly of the anonymous: Who am I?

Christmas Eve

Erect capital's arch;
decorate it with the gilt edge
of the moon. Pave the way to it
with cheques and with credit –

it is still not high enough
for the child to pass under
who comes to us this midnight
invisible as radiation.

The Lost

We are the lost people.
Tracing us by our language
you will not arrive where we are
which is nowhere. The wind
blows through our castles; the chair
of poetry is without a tenant.
We are exiles within
our own country; we eat our bread
at a pre-empted table. 'Show us,'
we supplicate, 'the way home',
and they laughing hiss at us:
'But you are home. Come in
and endure it.' Will nobody
explain what it is like
to be born lost? We have our signposts
but they are in another tongue.
If we follow our conscience
it leads us nowhere but to gaol.
The ground moves under our feet;
our one attitude is vertigo.
'And a little child,' the Book tells us
'shall lead them.' But this one
has a linguistic club
in his hand with which, old as we are,
he trounces and bludgeons us senseless.

S.K.

Like Christ we know little
of him when he was young.

Did he, as Yeats did, gather
actual shells on a cold shore?

Peering into a Danish mist
we discover no manger

to which the wise brought their gifts,
although myrrh would have been fitting.

Who were his teachers? He learned
his anonymity from God himself,

leaving his readers, as God
leaves the reader in life's

book to grope for the meaning
that will be quicksilver in the hand.

    'Kiss me, kiss me not.'
    'I love you, I reject you' –
    The game was perilous
    to them both, though her

    wound was for stanching
    as his own was not.
    His gaiety in public
    was a shirt of nettles for him

    at night. Hapless Regine
    with her moonlight hair,
    how was she to guess no apparent
    lunatic was ever more sane?

He was the first
of the Surrealists, picturing
our condition with the draughtsmanship

of a Dalí, but under
a pseudonym always.
The limpidity of his prose

had a cerebral gloss
prohibitive of transparence.
His laughter was that

of an author out of the asylum
of his genius. Imagining
from his emphasis on the self

that God is not other,
we are arrested by his shadow
in which the face of the beloved

is as a candle snuffed out
in the darkness following
on the mind's dazzling explosion.

Either way there was terror.
Backwards there was the moor
in Jutland, where his father,

from the Calvary of himself,
had accused God. Forward
there was the one overtaken

by his own speed, thought
brought to bay by a truth
as inscrutable as its reflection.

How do we know his study
was not the garden
over again, where his mind
was the serpent, insinuator
of the heresy of the self
as God? The difficulty
with prayer is the exchange
of places between I and thou,
with silence as the answer
to an imagined request.
Is this the price genius
must pay, that from an emphasis
on the subjective only
soliloquy remains? Is prayer
not a glass that, beginning
in obscurity as his books
do, the longer we stare
into the clearer becomes
the reflection of a countenance
in it other than our own?

The Pearl

'I think we have not,'
I said, 'been introduced.'

'No need,' it replied;
'I introduced myself

in the Garden, metallic
of scale, offering

the future to you in place
of the god's past. Would you

grow wings, anticipate
the clock? Behold, I am

at your door, in your
kitchen, at your bed's

side. I was the irritant
in the oyster that was

Leonardo's brain you have
split open to prove

to your conditioned audience
there is no pearl without price.'

Evening

The archer with time
as his arrow – has he broken
his strings that the rainbow
is so quiet over our village?

Let us stand, then, in the interval
of our wounding, till the silence
turn golden and love is
a moment eternally overflowing.

Parables

Asking love to entertain a belief
in it with promises of betrayal.

Why criticise? There always have been
queues of the imaginatively unemployed.

'There is a conscientious objection to peace, too,'
the strong testify at history's tribunal.

'Freedom is any direction we choose,'
the fish claim in the net drawing them.

The priest's cure, not on prescription, is
that love's casualties must be mended by love.

Then

The bone's song will be:
'Let me sleep. I am not
Yeats. I cannot face
over again the coming
of the machine. What was it
but a twig put in our hands
for the divining of the blood's
mineral within the marrow?'

And the one who is used
to ignoring prayer
will put the bone to his lips,
blowing it to the dust
that dances before
the galaxies, casting its veils
one by one to emerge
beautiful and deadly
as the nuclear core
that, Narcissus-like,
he gazes upon
as though it were a mirror.

Riposte

'A matter of chance?'
'All right for the lucky.

For those born blind,
those whom the crab

mumbles.' 'A design, then?'
'Not orientated manward.'

'Are you brave? Is life
but a sea, golden-

winged, moulting
upon our shores to

develop new feathers
for its meaningless returns?'

'You would persuade me
toward God.' 'What God?

Are we apparel
of his wardrobe, clothes

to be worn an hour
in a procession and cast off?'

'You make a mountain
of a concept. Why is there not

level ground, where
the rankness of evil

falls to our paternosters?'
'You derive vocabulary

from the Schoolmen.
Omnipotence is no answer

to secondary causation.'
'All right, I allow

you your mountain,
if you will allow

me that the cloud
at its summit is what

God withdraws into
at the moment of illumination.'

To a Lady

I don't know
who I write to,
the frocked girl,
pretty but pert,
or the grown-up
mother, doll-less
but dolled. Nor
does death either
who, liquidating
her lungs, applying
irons to her heart,
discovers, astonished,
a being somewhere
between both, perter
than a child, prettier
than a parent, and
wiser than each
of them in the way
she treats his fumbling
familiarity with contempt.

Afallon

It is Adam's other
kingdom, what he might have
inherited had he
refused the apple, the nuclear
fruit with the malignant core.
Its women trace their descent
not to Eve but to Lilith,
the spirit that whispers to us
when we take the world
in our arms. Standing
under the tree of man,
our roots in the soil, we listen
to Rhiannon's birds high
in the branches, calling to us
to forget time, so that the heart
answers: Its lichened manuscripts
of stone; its wind-laundered
clouds; the moving
staircases of its streams –
the traveller gets down
onto a midnight platform
and knows from the rustle
of unseen water-
falls he has come home.
Once our literature
was on the continent's
lips; we exchanged delegates
with its princes. In a world
oscillating between dollar
and yen our liquidities
are immaterial. We
continue our relationship
with the young David, flooring
the cheque-book giant
with one word taken,
smooth as a pebble, out
of the brook of our language.

Wrong?

Where is that place apart
you summon us to? Noisily
we seek it and have no time
to stay. Stars are distant;
is it more distant still,
out in the dark in the shadow
of thought itself? No wonder
it recedes as we calculate
its proximity in light years.

Maybe we were mistaken
at the beginning or took later
a wrong turning. In curved space
one can travel for ever and not recognise
one's arrivals. I feel rather
you are at our shoulder, whispering
of the still pool we could sit down
by; of the tree of quietness
that is at hand; cautioning us
to prepare not for the breathless journeys
into confusion, but for the stepping
aside through the invisible
veil that is about us into a state
not place of innocence and delight.

Still

You waited with impatience
each year for the autumn migration.
It happened and was over.

Your turn then. You departed,
not southward into the burnished
and sunlit country, but out

into the dark, where there are
no poles, no accommodating
horizons. Last night, as I loitered

where your small bones had their nest,
the owl blew away from your stone cross
softly as down from a thistle-head. I wondered.

Meteorological

It was always weather.
The reason of our being
was to record it, telling it
how it was hot, cold, wet
to the pointlessness of saturation.
It was a disposition
of the impersonal, an expression
on what could have been
blank space. It repeated itself
in a way we were never tired
of listening to. 'Do that again,'
we implored it on the morrow
of a fine day. When it was grey
you could have described it
as sullen. On sparkling mornings
it flashed us smile after smile so
we became familiar with it.
It breathed then into our very being
refrigerating us. To curse it
was to have it regard us
out of the mildest of skies,
fondling us with the wind's
tapering fingers. They say
it was like this before
our arrival. How could it
have been without us
to convince it? What, when we
have gone, will become
of it, endlessly occurring
over our vocabulary's Sahara?

Heretics

All congregate;
all murmur an Amen
to the prayers. The preacher
deviates within narrowing
parameters. They were born
in sight of the one church;
they have to lie in its shadow.
Man has to believe
something. May as well invest
in this creed as in that.
Parthenogenesis! the door was flung
open to proliferation:
Nicaea, Chalcedon. The divine
blood dried in the libraries;
but the pages formicated
with the contradictory words.
The preacher scales unbelievable
heights by the bones of the martyrs.
What would his listeners
die for? Are they selective
like me, knowing that among
a myriad disciplines each one
has its orthodoxy from which
the words flow? Alas, we are heretics
all, and the one we subscribe to
is not love any more than the kingdom
for the sake of which we are
fools is the kingdom of heaven.

Illusory Arrival

Who was the janitor
with the set face, wardening
the approaches? I had prepared
my apologies, my excuses

for coming by the wrong
road. There was no one
there, only the way
I had come by going on and on.

Reflections

The furies are at home
in the mirror; it is their address.
Even the clearest water,
if deep enough can drown.

Never think to surprise them.
Your face approaching ever
so friendly is the white flag
they ignore. There is no truce

with the furies. A mirror's temperature
is always at zero. It is ice
in the veins. Its camera
is an X-ray. It is a chalice

held out to you in
silent communion, where gaspingly
you partake of a shifting
identity never your own.

Nuance

With the cathedrals thundering
at him, history proving
him the two-faced god, there were
the few who waited on him
in the small hours, undaunted
by the absence of an echo
to their Amens. Physics' suggestion
is they were not wrong. Reality
is composed of waves and particles
coming at us as the Janus-faced
chooses. We must not despair.
The invisible is yet susceptible
of being inferred. To pray, perhaps, is
to have a part in an infinitesimal deflection.

No Time

She left me. What voice
colder than the wind
out of the grave said:
'It is over'? Impalpable,
invisible, she comes
to me still, as she would
do, and I at my reading.
There is a tremor
of light, as of a bird crossing
the sun's path, and I look
up in recognition
of a presence in absence.
Not a word, not a sound,
as she goes her way,
but a scent lingering
which is that of time immolating
itself in love's fire.

No Jonahs

What do the whales say
calling to one another
on their extended wave-lengths?
Why suppose that it is language?
It is pain searching for
an echo. It is regret
for a world that has men
in it. Shadows are without
weight in water yet bleed
their litres to the harpoon.
They have reversed human
history, so that land
is the memory of whence
they once came. They are drawn
to it to drown, as we are
to the sea. Their immense
brain cannot save them;
can ours, launching us
into fathomless altitudes, save us?

Incarnations

A child's memories
are of the womb, the sleep
by unearthly waters;
his dreams are of a happiness
unfounded. This one fell,
was torn out of a vast side
by envy in transit.
His whickering disordered
the stars, then silence took over,
twelve dawdling years
on the way to the temple.

　　　Take one from one
　　　there remain three.
　　　No, no, no.

　　　Through a child's answer
　　　a cross was drawn
　　　by Judaic fingers.

　　　The way forward
　　　was the way back
　　　to a carpenter's patience.

A preacher's temptation
is the voice persuading
he is his own message.
So the emphasis on the other
proved to them he blasphemed.
This stripling, this Nazarene
nobody the mirror
of God! They hurled their scorn's
stones and the cracks accentuated
the sky's age. There was scant time.
He withdrew into the wilderness
of the spirit. The true fast
was abstention from language.

He returned hungry
yet offered his body
as bread to believers.

The crumbs flew
lavishing their feathers
on twelve baskets.

They lost him then
in the garden of himself
gloomy with prayer

until Judas found him,
enviously guided by the sour
shining of his starved kiss.

What are a god's dreams?
Can he dream without sleep?
What was the Incarnation
but the waking dream of one
calling himself Son of Man?

For the dreams come, always they come:
the babe's dream by amniotic
waters; dream of the ovum
of the enchanted circle
when it was yet unpierced.

What are a child's dreams?
Bubbles blown for adults
to seek their reflections in?
What are the leaves in autumn
but the mind flaking beneath

truth's chisel? I have heard the professor,
laying his books down, huskily
describing the first rise
on a river in Scotland.
I have listened to the poet

with uncombed hair, delicate
of finger, adding nought
after nought to his imagined
balance. I have said to the future:
'Show me the dreamless man,

the prose man, the man imprisoned
by his horizons.' And the machine
stalled at an abyss, empty
as the tomb in Palestine,
the eternal afterdraught of the bone's dream.

Symbols

Always in my dream
he kneels there silently
writing upon the ground
what I can't read – signs
and diagrams; and his accusers
have withdrawn. He was with the future
always, but warning of it,
too. They were dependent
on language to inflict on him woe,
its old-fashioned artillery
hauled into place, firing
word after word at him
as he went on prophesying
their ultimate destruction.
It is true, our larynxes
are becoming rusty. The computer
can do things as fast,
faster. Vocabulary toils
breathlessly in the wake of contrived
objects. Yet he consented
to be hung up on one
of these same symbols,
knowing that their deployment was
synonymous with the death of the poem.

Circles

The astronauts could not conceal
their triumph. As the last star
drifted away on the port bow,
limitless space took them
to itself; weightlessness
possessed them. No hunger
anymore, no desire
for liquid. Immortality
was within their grasp as
an ability to travel
onward for ever. After how many
days? years? their instruments
were alerted; a forgotten gravity
began drawing them down to where
they had set forth. With a bleak
gleam the knowledge broke
on them that infinity also
was round. On a pitiless
runway no wives, children
awaited their return. Only the old
senators, statesmen were lined up
in their funereal clothing, ready
as ever to declare war.

The Case

'Where were you on the night of June 10?'
(Who is you? What does
the night of June 10 mean?
They are waiting for an answer.)
'I don't know any more
than you.'
                    'But we do know.
You were in bed with Siân Puw,
a child fifteen years old.'
(In bed! Ah, if I knew
what that meant. Is it their word
for love? She leaned over me
and I saw through her hair
the stars thawing. A nightjar rang
in the fern, an electric bell
whose battery had not run down
millions of years.)
                    'Siân Puw?
I know of no such person.'
                              'Look
at this. Do you declare the writing
is not yours?'
                  (So they can forge
and get away with it!)
                          'Give
me a pen and I will show you
that everything my hand touches
is poetry.'
              'Silence. Any more laughter
and I will have the court cleared.
Now, prisoner, will you answer
the question: Where were you
on the night of June 10?'
                            (So
this is the wheel on which
all are broken. Round and round
until you give them the answer
they wish to hear, so they can go home

to bed and bring their wives round
to the point they have brought me,
where from weariness they reply:
All right; it is as you say;
the person you call me
is in bed with him whom you call
you. Let us perpetrate
a marriage.)
                    'But,' I cry,
as they lead me away
'the stars have gone out in their curling-pinned
hair, and the nightjar has shorted.'

At the End

Few possessions: a chair,
a table, a bed
to say my prayers by,
and, gathered from the shore,
the bone-like, crossed sticks
proving that nature
acknowledges the Crucifixion.
All night I am at
a window not too small
to be frame to the stars
that are no further off
than the city lights
I have rejected. By day
the passers-by, who are not
pilgrims, stare through the rain's
bars, seeing me as prisoner
of the one view, I who
have been made free
by the tide's pendulum truth
that the heart that is low now
will be at the full tomorrow.

A Species

Shipwrecked upon an island
in a universe whose tides
are the winds, they began multiplying
without joy. They cut down the trees
to have room to make money.

The one who is without name,
but all-powerful, sowed intelligence
in them like a virus. As living room
became scarce, as rain became acid,
they became conscious there were other islands

all round, garlands hung up
at the festivities of science,
waiting to be colonised not by
the imagination but in fact.
They learned how time can be superannuated

by speed, making an archipelago
of the stars, hurrying from one
to another with their infection.
There came a day when the one
without name and whose signature

is in cypher willed them to go back
to their first home, destitute but wiser.
They turned as to a familiar, seeing it
for the first time, suspended in beauty,
blue with cold, but waiting to be loved.

Runes

January had a sob in its throat;
it coughed it and February lay there frozen.

March began hoping for clean things
but April bleared it with its catarrh.

May called to the year to come dancing
but June freckled its dress with blood.

That which was brought forth sprawling in July
died in August among the corn stalks.

In September the fox hid in the bracken
fearing the horn of the October moon.

November arrived with its present of gold leaves
for the child-like snow in its December cradle.

Mischief

'Oh,' he said, 'I have lived with nothingness
so long it has lost its meaning.
I have said "yes" to the universe
so many times its echoes
have returned increasingly as "no".
I have developed my negatives
of the divine and preserved their technicolour
in a make-believe album. I realise
the imagination is alive only
in an oxygenated world. The truth
is less breath-taking than the vacuum
into which it withdraws. But against
all this I have seen the lamb
gambolling for a moment, as though
life were a good thing. This, I have said,
is God's roguery, juggling
with the scales, weighting the one
pan down with evil piled
upon evil then sending it suddenly
sky-high with in the other a tear
fallen from the hardest of eyes.

Near and Far

No one so busy
as you are. Where is that
seventh day when you rest
from your labour? I arise
from sleep to find that
you have been all night growing.
And by day you are abroad
endlessly exploring a circumference
by which you are not confined.
You have no words yet vibrate
in me with the resonance of an Amen.
You are strung with light
as with nerves across which
thought is drawn to deliver
intellectual music. Sometimes
you are an impulse upon my walls,
at others a modifying
of unseen organisms, slowly
and delicately as a mutation;
but always as far off
as you are near, terrifying
me as much by your proximity
as by your being light-years away.

Resurrections

Easier for them, God
only at the beginning
of his recession. Blandish him,
said the times and they did so,
Herbert, Traherne, walking
in a garden not yet
polluted. Music in Donne's
mind was still polyphonic.

The corners of the spirit waiting
to be developed, Hopkins
renewed the endearments
taming the lion-like presence
lying against him. What
happened? Suddenly he was
gone, leaving love guttering
in his withdrawal. And scenting
disaster, as flies are attracted
to a carcase, far down
in the subconscious the ghouls
and the demons we thought
we had buried for ever resurrected.

The Indians and the Elephant

'It is like a tree,'
the blind Indian cried
encountering the beast's trunk.
'Like a rope, I would say,'
cried another, discovering
its tail. I, though I am
not blind, feel my way
about God, exploring him
in darkness. Sometimes he is
a wind, carrying me off;
sometimes a fire devouring
me. Rarely, too rarely
he is as the scent
at the heart of a great flower
I lean over and fall
into. But always he surrounds
me, mostly as a cloud
lowering, but one through which
suddenly light will strike,
burnishing the cross
waiting on me with spread wings
like the fiercest of raptors.

Swallows

To the swallows:
'See you next year.'
These swallows? No
matter. On the wires
will be swallows, the music
of time in customary
notation. Not like
me whose migrations
are endless, though my perch
be of bone. One April
I will return to it
no more. As nature
replaces its creatures
so life will replace
me, a migrant
between nominatives,
a new singer of an old
song, an innovator
too regardless of time
for the time-keeping swallows.

Negative

One word. Say it.
'No.' No is the word, then?
'No,' Stevens misled us.
We are waiting and the 'yes'
has not come. But the dawn
has come and already
the day heads towards night.

Her name was Rhiannon.
Time ceased as I listened.
Yet when silence fell
on her birds I was old.
Trees that were once green
had turned into chimneys
and the Minotaur's breath

soured the land. A child came
and what I thought in his hand
was the key to the kingdom
turned into a retort
and test-tube, and his caliper eyes
were being stretched for measuring
the widening gap between love and money.

Winged God

All men. Or shall we say,
not chauvinistic, all
people, it is all
people? Beasts manure
the ground, nibble to
promote growth; but man,
the consumer, swallows
like the god of mythology
his own kind. Beasts walk
among birds and never
do the birds scare; but the human,
that alienating shadow
with the Bible under the one
arm and under the other
the bomb, as often
drawn as he is repelled
by the stranger waiting for him
in the mirror – how
can he return home
when his gaze forages
beyond the stars? Pity him,
then, this winged god, rupturer
of gravity's control
accelerating on and
outward in the afterglow
of a receding laughter?

Raptor

You have made God small,
setting him astride
a pipette or a retort
studying the bubbles,
absorbed in an experiment
that will come to nothing.

I think of him rather
as an enormous owl
abroad in the shadows,
brushing me sometimes
with his wing so the blood
in my veins freezes, able

to find his way from one
soul to another because
he can see in the dark.
I have heard him crooning
to himself, so that almost
I could believe in angels,

those feathered overtones
in love's rafters, I have heard
him scream, too, fastening
his talons in his great
adversary, or in some lesser
denizen, maybe, like you or me.

X Loves Y

We went to the same school.
Shall I telephone her
now? 'This is Mortimer
speaking from fifty
years off. Can you hear me?
Are you beautiful
still? Dare I venture
to come up to your front
door, with you opening
it and I enquiring
for you? You say my voice
is the same. Are you a chord
I struck that has not ceased
its vibrations, so you can tune
my changes to it?

Supposing I come
and we meet by the tree
we carved our symbols on,
is this the completion
of our education – two
heads in pupilage
to two hearts with time's
arrow piercing them?'

Boundaries

Where does the town end
and the country begin?

Where is the high-water mark
between the grey tide and the green?

We walk an invisible margin
remembering glory,

when the labourer was no more
than knee-deep in his acres

and looked up at the sound of the bell
of the worshipping cathedral.

The country has ebbed over
the centuries, taking the town with it,

and now the town welcomes itself back,
time's castaway floundering amid the jetsam.

Incubation

In the absence of such wings
as were denied us we insist
on inheriting others from the machine.
The eggs that we incubate bring forth
in addition to saints monsters,
the featherless brood whose one thing
in common with dunnocks is
that they do not migrate. We are fascinated
by evil; almost you could say
it is the plumage we acquire
by natural selection. There is a contradiction
here. Generally subdued feathers
in birds are compensated for
by luxuriant song. Not so these
whose frayed notes go with their plain clothes.
It is we who, gaudy as jays,
make cacophonous music under an egg-shell sky.

The Mass of Christ

This day I am with the beasts –
animal Christmas – staring
with brute eyes at the mystery
in the cradle. Emmanuel!
God with men, but not God
with the creatures. Are we in need
of a saviour, when it is not
our fault? Nebuchadnezzar,
the beasts' Christ, incarnate
as an animal and not
as a human being, but with a human
conscience. What love sentenced
us to murder in order
that we survive? Does God know
what it is to eat his food
off the ground, to draw sustenance
from intestines? We prey
and are preyed on. Such peace
as we know is purchased
only by an interminable
alertness. When winter arrives
we lie out in the open country
because we have to, wrapping
our threadbare breath about our
aggrieved bones. Does God die
and still live? We live only
by the perpetual sacrifice
of our kind, ignorant
of love, yet innocent of a love
that has anthropomorphised its creation.

Gwladus Ddu

(from the Welsh of G.J. Williams)

It was an old white-friar who wrote
on yellowing parchment among tales
of the Welsh princes these words:
'That year was buried Gwladus Ddu.'

What was it made a brother
in his cell insert this in his story?
Did he taste heaven once in seeing
the sun brighten the darkness of Gwladus Ddu?

And I, too, by my fireside remembered,
seeing Eryri's cover white as wool,
that seven hundred winters had grizzled it
since summer basked in the hair of Gwladus Ddu.

Just now behind the manuscript's account
of old, bold knights I saw a face
bloodless and unsmiling and the words:
'That year was buried Gwladus Ddu.'

Neither

Not a person, neither
less than, since we are so,
personal. Impassible
yet darkening your countenance
once for a long moment
as you looked at yourself
on a hill-top in Judea.
Your mastery is to be both
outside and inside, standing off
from the primary explosion,
entering in to its quieter
repetitions in acorn and spermatozoa.
You have given us the ability
to ask the unanswerable question,
to have glimpses of you
as you were, only to stand dumb
at the limits of our articulation.
Is it our music interprets you
best, a heart-beat at the very centre
of your creation? Is it art,
depicting man's figure as the conductor
to your lightning? Had I
the right words, it is the poem
that would announce you to
an amazed audience; no longer
a linguistic wrestling but a signal
projected at you and returning quick
with the unpredictabilities at your centre.

The Promise

Promising myself before bedtime
to contend more urgently
with the problem. From nothing
nothing comes. Behind everything –
something, somebody? In the beginning
violence, the floor of the universe
littered with fragments. After
that enormous brawl, where
did the dove come from? From what
acorn mind these dark
boughs among which at night
thought loses its way back
to its dim sources, onward
to that illuminated citadel
that truth keeps? Light's distances
are without meaning and unreconciled
by the domestic. I pit my furniture
against the emptiness that is beyond
Antares, but the equation
is not in balance. There are no cushions
for the emotions. Thermodynamic
cold or else incineration
of the planet – either way
there is no hope for the species.
Are Sophocles and Mozart sufficient
justification for the failure
to find out? Beyond
the stars are more stars where love, perhaps,
or intellect or the anonymous is busy.

Two Shirts on a Line

They set to one another
then move silently
apart only to return
back to back. I am
fascinated by a dance
without music, by
a couple without faces
dancing away a January
morning, drying
their tears. There is no one
to put them on but
the wind that fits them
where it touches,
that, when about to be
asked for directions, vanishes
leaving them dangling
as though they had been hanged.

Bird Watching

Choosing amid many whisperings
the enamel platitudes
of the Mediterranean; Sappho
and Propertius at it
to impinge on the *Telegraph*'s
stop press; to observe birds
their wavering italics
in competition with the ocean's
serene gaze. The post chaise
was a necessary adjunct
of the grand tour; we thumb
our way, our arrival
as unsuspected as an occurrence
of influenza. A thousand
binoculars winnow
the thin haze. Eyes
that in other places
would be penetrating
the young women's amorphous
clothing can here notice
the lack of cosmetics
that distinguish one warbler
from another. Winged God
approve that in a world
that has appropriated flight
to itself there are still people
like us, who believe
in the ability of the heart
to migrate, if only momentarily,
between the quotidian and the sublime.

Homage to Wallace Stevens

I turn now
not to the Bible
but to Wallace Stevens.
Insured against
everything but the muse
what has the word-wizard
to say? His adjectives
are the wand he waves
so language gets up
and dances under
a fastidious moon.
We walk a void world,
he implies for which
in the absence of the imagination,
there is no hope. Verbal bank-clerk,
acrobat walking a rhythmic tight-rope,
trapeze artist of the language
his was a kind of double-entry
poetics. He kept two columns
of thought going, balancing meaning
against his finances. His poetry
was his church and in it
curious marriages were conducted.
He burned his metaphors like incense,
so his syntax was as high
as his religion.
    Blessings, Stevens;
I stand with my back to grammar
at an altar you never aspired
to, celebrating the sacrament
of the imagination whose high-priest
notwithstanding you are.

Hallowe'en

Outside a surfeit of planes.
Inside the hunger of the departed
to come back. 'Ah, erstwhile humans,
would you make your mistakes
over again? In life, as in love,
the second time round is
no better.'
　　　　　　I confront their expressions
in the embers, on grey walls:
faces among the stones watching
me to see if this night
of all nights I will make sacrifice
to the spirits of hearth and of
roof-tree, pouring a libation.

'Stay where you are,' I implore.
'This is no world for escaped beings
to make their way back into.
The well that you took your pails
to is polluted. At the centre
of the mind's labyrinth the machine howls
for the sacrifice of the affections;
vocabulary has on a soft collar
but the tamed words are not to be trusted.
As long as the flames hum, making
their honey, better to look in
upon truth's comb than to
take off as we do on fixed wings
for depollinated horizons.'

The Waiting

Are there angels or only
the Furies? We sleep
on a stone pillow
and the troubles of Europe
are the molecules that
compound it. Where is
the ladder or that heavenly
traffic that electrified Jacob?

We wrestle with somebody,
something which withholds its name.
How is the anonymous
disposed? The enemy is without
number; is there an infiltration
of its forces by one not
indifferent to the human?
Though genes have their war,

yet the smiling goes on
from cradle to cradle.
Our experiments are repeatable,
but what is love the precipitate
of? We have eaten of a tree
whose foliage is radioactive
and the autumn of
its fall-out is upon our children.

Why, then, of all possible
turnings do we take
this one rather than that,
when the only signs discernible
are what no one has erected?
Is it because, at the road's
ending, the one who is as a power
in hiding is waiting to be christened?

Navigation

(for Lee McOwan)

There go the storeyed liners,
the tankers, the thudding substitutes
for the billowing schooners
that were blown away as though
they were time's clouds. I wave
to them on their way – where?
They are, as I am, outward
bound over multitudinous
fathoms. The crew lean over
the taffrail, I over myself
and suffer the old nausea
of the unknown. Sometimes when there is
fog, I hear the horn calling
to them to be careful. When I
kneel down in the obscurity
that is God, there is no comparable
voice, however melancholy,
to direct me.
             Never mind,
traveller, there are the heights,
too, where the intellect
meets with God in its own
weather. By day I see the 'planes
reflecting him with the clarity
that is thought. By night
their instruments deputise
for him and are unerring.
God, on this latest stage
of my journey let me profit
from my inventions by christening
them yours. Amid the shoals and hazards
that are about me, let me employ
radar as though it were your gift.

Nant Gwrtheyrn

I listen to the echoes
of John Jones crying: 'God
is not good,' and of his wife
correcting him: 'Hush, John.'

'The cuckoo returns
to Gwrtheyrn, contradicting
John Jones, within its voice
bluebells tolling over

the blue sea. There is work
here still, quarrying
for an ancient language
to bring it to the light

from under the years'
dust covering it. Men,
with no palate for fine
words, they helped them down

with their sweat, spitting
them out later in what
served them for prayer. Was
it for this God numbered

their days? Where once pick-
axes would question, now
only the stream ticks, telling
a still time to listeners

at their text-books. Turning
its back on the world,
contemplating without boredom
unchanging horizons this place

knows a truth, for here
is the resurrection
of things. One after one
they arise in answer

to names they are called by,
standing around, shining,
by brief graves from whose hold
willing hands have released them.

Bestiary

Owl

The owl has a clock's
face, but there is no time
on it. No raptor ever
is half-past its prey.

The talons revolve
and the beak strikes the
twelve sharp notes that are
neither midday nor midnight

on the skull's anvil
but links of a chain
that thought forges and thought
tries continually to break.

Mice

I am an impressed
audience. Their whiskers
are finer than the strings
of a violin. They turn over
the pages of an unseen
score. They have teeth,
too, smaller than rice
with which they gnaw
and gnaw, as the mind gnaws
at the truth. I lie awake
listening to them, asking
myself would I come
at the truth, coming later
where they have been
at work? A rodent
is a tireless reminder
to the mind worrying away
that the end of such performance
is to bring the house down.

Mosquito

A crane, a miniature
sheerlegs with no
load but infection

tuned to inaudible
decibels laying
earth's civilisations

in ruins stopped in flight
by the brittle unbreakable
noose of the spider.

Snake

I came on the adder
with its doll's eyes
patently smiling and

as if it were a toy
in the earth's nursery
tried playing with it

only to find that although
still as a stopped clock
it was still ready to strike.

Goat

A glass eye
it sees everything
with. A file on iron
for conversation and
the cloven foot
relating it to the devil.
We think we keep it
on a precise tether
but arriving find
that everything is eaten
so re-provision
it. We can't let
even the evil one
starve itself to death.

Tiger

The tiger at the zoo
like earthed lightning
its concertina face

opening and closing
on the rasped bone
its asthmatic music.

Bear

The bear cuddly
by a tamed fire
but out in the wild

making to all
our attempts at familiarity
its crushing replies.

Lizard

Green jewel, minute
basilisk, trigger cocked
on the sunned stone in readiness
to go off, I put you out

with my shadow, think
to ignite you again
by withdrawing but
you are not there

anymore, you have shot
yourself into oblivion, leaving
me with not a thing to remember
but the silence of your explosion.

Barn Owl

The owl calls.
It is not Yeats'
owl; it moves
not in circles

but direct through
the ear to the heart,
refrigerating it.
It belongs not

to the mind's order.
It was that which perched
on the boneless arm
of the scarecrow

that life had set
up to keep death off.
As a poet I am
dumb; as painter

my brush would shrivel
in its acetylene
eyes. What, as composer,
could I do but mimic

its deciduous notes
flaking from it
with a feather's softness
but as frigidly as snow?

Guests

As though a trumpet were blown
I was immediately aware
of her presence: a weeping willow
uprooted, a girl with hair
pouring; the sort of helplessness
that commands; eyes smouldering
from an imagined insult. Such
women are always alone
with their escort. This one, her
latest, was trying to ignore
the looks that ignored him.
Dressed all in black, but
correctly, what in the wincing light
off her bare shoulders could he
ever appear to be but her shadow?

Le Dormeur du Val

In the beginning
the word. Will the word
be at the end?

At the end
by the dried-up
river of our inventions

I think the computer
will lie, worsted
by meaning, with civilisation's

two small holes
in its side, done for
like time's soldier

and as speechless,
but unable to stanch
the haemorrhage of its figures.

Homage to Paul Klee

An egg with spectacles
on. The full moon
come down to walk
a trapeze. And thought
weightless, balancing itself
in scale-pans. We are
amused by such insouciance
in art. The errors
of centuries begin peeling
from museum walls.
Love after all was nothing
but man tantalising
himself with time's arrow.
See here how easily
the ridiculous establishes itself
as existing without end.

Lest thought
take itself seriously
he put on it toy
hats, balanced it
on a tight-rope, gave theorems
a music to which
surds danced. His lines
were an insect's limbs.
Often, looking at
his drawings, I imagined
an expression only to find
it was the concern
of angles with their degrees.

With the mind of an insect
reducing the problem
to which of his feet
to put forth first, keeping
a time that is more music
than progress, scribbling,
where once there was crucifixion,
those crotchets and semiquavers
with which levity begins.

The Elusive

What time is it on a face?
It is eternity on this one
that I try to recall
by humming; but I am out of tune.
It is the face of the woman
in the valley of Sorek.
I listen to its adagio.
I will make many poems
in her honour, all of them failures.
Dante, what would you have done?
ap Gwilym, Catullus?
                                    I have waited
for her to emerge on the pavement
of everyday, but the traffic erased her.
There must be an exit by which
she escapes into those unbuilt
areas of the imagination, where sense
must give way to thought and thought
to repining. I have said on my knees
I want nothing of her
but to behold her. Is there no place
in my mind for her replica
to be hung up, so I may visit her
at will and replenish my thirst
at her sources?
                                    She is life's gage
flung down the muse must bend
to pick up, never succeeding.
I would put her in a boat
of clean sails and steer
towards an island unvisited
by death. But humbler than I,
wiser, she is content to walk
birdless streets and be served
for much money with cheap
goods and return with them
to a small house, perhaps in this town,
and children of human seed.

The Morrow

That day after the night death;
that night after the day's wailing,
I went out on the hill
and contemplated the lit windows
and the stars, those flocks
without a shepherd; and I asked:
'Is she up there, the woman
who was the pawn that love
offered in exchange for beauty?'

Later I was alone in my room
reading and, the door closed,
she was there, speechlessly enquiring:
Was all well? It was true
what the book said in answer
to the world's question as to where
at death does the soul go:
'There is no need under a pillarless
heaven for it to go anywhere.'

Remembering

Love her now
      for her ecstasies,
her willingness to oblige.
There will come a time
she will show her love for you
         in her cooking,
her sewing; in a bed made up
      for passionless sleeping.

The wrinkles will come upon her
      calm though her brow be
under time's blowing. Frost will visit
      her hair's midnight and not
thaw. Her eyes that were a fine day
         will cloud over
      and rain down desultory
tears when, as she infers,
you are not looking. Your part then
will be to take her hand in your
      hand, proving to her
that, if blind, it is not dumb.

Island

I would still go there
if only to await
the once-in-a-lifetime
opening of truth's flower;

if only to escape
such bought freedom, and live,
prisoner of the keyless sea,
on the mind's bread and water.

Portraits

1

He has ears and is not
deaf. Why do I have to shout?
Is there need for the breaking
of ground for meaning to enter?
The skull is of bark; the ears
are overgrown with lichen.
A stranger to language
that rises above the level
of the primaeval, he would not
recognise himself in the mirror
of a technology that was held
up to him. This is a face come on
in the museum of the species
that you must travel as far
back to converse with as the owner
must come forward to confront you.

2

Ordinary but elusive,
with something of the squirrel
about her in the way
she gathers her eyes' hazels

and plays with them before you.
But a bird; too, a suggestion
of feathers and a willingness
to alight on one's second thoughts.

No words too ponderous
but to be sent packing by her
into the rumours where they belong.
If we would feed her language

it must be fine seed as sunny
as her nature, which can
accept nothing from us but
such as enables her to sing.

3

There before you have done
speaking, persuading
difficulty to be something
which you imagine. A wearer
of dark glasses to protect
you against his cleverness's
glare, or to dilute
the blush that suffuses
you on being so understood.

No fists, no
biceps, but this
is the descendant of David
who, with steel pebbles
taken from the mind's brook
has for ever laid
low the muscle-bound,
close-quarters club–
wielder whose aim is
to hold the intelligence in thrall.

Vespers

Listen, I have a song
to sing that time will
punish you for listening
to and you will not know it.

There was a woman
of few years and strange
name who was the apple
in my garden I reached

for and could not gather.
So I went forth into
the world seeking for
her equal, and came

back navigating by
her quick compass to learn,
looking at her, how
I was old now and she fair still.

Silence

The relation between us was
silence; that and the feeling
of each one being watched
by the other: I by an
enormous pupil in a blank
face, he by one in a million
wanderers in the darkness
that was never a long way off
from his presence.
                    It had begun
by my talking all of the time
repeating the worn formulae
of the churches in the belief
that was prayer. Why does silence
suggest disapproval? The prattling
ceased, not suddenly but,
as flowers die off in a frost
my requests thinned. I contented
myself I was answering
his deafness with dumbness. My tongue
lolled, clapper of a disused
bell that would never again
pound on him.
                    What are the emotions
of God? There was no admiring
of my restraint, no suggestion even
of a recompense for my patience.
If he had allowed himself but one
word: his name, for instance, spoken
ever so obliquely; my own that,
for all his majesty, acknowledged
my existence.
                    And yet there were creatures
around me with their ears
pricked; figures on ancient cathedrals,
the denizens of art, with their rapt,
innocent faces and heads on one side
as though they were listening. Ah, but to whom?

Blind Noel

Christmas; the themes are exhausted.
Yet there is always room
on the heart for another
snowflake to reveal a pattern.

Love knocks with such frosted fingers.
I look out. In the shadow
of so vast a God I shiver, unable
to detect the child for the whiteness.

Words

Accuse me of sincerity
I deny complicity
art is my necessity.

Is there a conspiracy
against sagacity?
Confound simplicity.

Not electricity
but the brush's piety
affords divinity.

Play

Jocosity
through verbosity
can lead to animosity,

as an attitude
from exactitude
can become a platitude.

Complementarity
leads not with the majority
to popularity,

as scrupulosity
has the capacity
to encourage pomposity.

Belief in the Trinity
for most of humanity
suggests a nonentity.

I fear theology
is just an allergy
of anthropology.

Heigh-ho that the universe
through over-rehearsal
should become farcical.

Relativity
in the face of gravity
is incivility.

In a Calvinist's heaven,
where no foot is cloven,
who are the forgiven?

Time does not prevaricate.
Where the heart pontificates
the questions proliferate.

Is not astrology
disguised as the economy
the human pathology?

One could go on and on
like the traffic in London –
It is late. I have done.

Anybody's Alphabet

All art is anonymous.
Listen: *Ai ee*; *ai ee*,
the unaspirated sound
out of a cave in anticipation
of human anguish, aftermath
of the alibis of God.

Beauty and the beast
bedded together, begotten
in one womb, battering
later at truth's bars,
beseeching precedence, both
badly bruised in the end.

Compulsion and choice,
contending champions;
co-respondents in a case
not for the courts;
curious as to whether free
one can be compelled to choose.

Dust and decay,
ditherers upon the doorstep
of death itself; dried-
up ghosts of daisy-chain
days that were once dappled
with dew and delight.

Except, then,
for electricity each
of us would be earthed
and effete, our light
like the evening star extinguished
for ever aeons ago.

For Stevens fictions
were as familiar
as facts and if far-
fetched preferable.
Forfeiting for faith
fable, he feasted on it.

God graven
erstwhile gives now
before mind's groping
after him among germs,
galaxies. Gone, he still
gazes upon us. Gracious.

As in Holland
on the horizontal hills
have to be conceived,
so heaven and hell
are hearsay only for those
held up half-way between.

The I as idea
incarnate, inimical
to the impartial, infinite
in the intensity of its
opposition to the incursions
of an implicit Thou.

Is not the judgment
of judicious men
that words beginning
with just j like jeering,
joking all of them put
the jewel-like spirit in jeopardy?

Kingly but not kind:
nature with its knowledge
of how to keep kith
and kin ready to kneel
down or keel over
at the dropping of its kerchief.

Lust and love, the mind's
Siamese twins
listening to each other
lying about life,
one leering, one laughing
in their loneliness together.

Maiden of many
motions, mahogany-
eyed, making with those same
movements as much
music for me as does
your mouth with its modes.

Needing to be neither
narrow nor nasty
to understand how
the neutrality of nice
men is not so much
non-combatant as it is naive.

Overtures of opportunity
or obsequies of the outworn?
Obols are obsolete now
for the oarsman through space-time;
the oracle not so much
out of order as it is out of date.

Particle physics provides
parallels with the Upanishads.
Today's prophet is preoccupied
with the present, that non-
point at which a paradoxical
future paves the way to the past.

In queenlier times
the quaint was the known quantity
the knight was in quest of.
In the age of the quark
the queer's quandary is
that he is not quite.

Is it right for the wrong
to be rich even if
ruefully? Are the real
rewards of romance
to be reaped only when reason
at long last is at rest?

Where is sincerity's sanction?
Six times out of seven
the slippery tongue is successful.
Blake's saying is a sure
stumbling block for simpletons
on their way to salvation.

True to type travelling
towards truth and turning
too often aside.
There are the thoroughfare
and the thousands of
no-through-roads which we take.

Universal understanding
unveiled. Unnecessary
anymore for the under-privileged,
the under-dog to sit up
and beg in the face of usury's
urge towards urbanisation.

Virtually a virgin.
Very well. But veering
towards vagueness, if questioned
on the value of the voluptuous
when no more than a veil
for the viciousness of a virago.

Windy and wet, and what is
worse the weather within
wicked: wounds and the heart's
woe, when all should be well.
Ah, waif spirit, will you not wake
once again to wonder and worship?

The xtremities of the Cross
so far xaggerated
as to become the kiss
of the xploiter, an xample
of how, when all things could
be xcellent, all are wrong.

You and I God – Yahweh,
the scientist's yogi –
youthful as tomorrow;
yawing but never yielding
to my yearning all these years
for myself to become you.

But east of Zion
there is Zen, that zone
where zeal can become
zest. On zany thermometers
then, the readings of the zeitgeist
are never at zero.

Selected Poems
1946-1968
BY
R.S. THOMAS

First published in 1973, this is R.S. Thomas's own selection from six of the finest books of poetry published since the war: *Song at the Year's Turning* (1955), *Poetry for Supper* (1958), *Tares* (1961), *The Bread of Truth* (1963), *Pietà* (1966) and *Not He That Brought Flowers* (1968). It includes many of his best-known poems, such as 'A Peasant', 'Welsh Landscape', 'Evans', 'On the Farm' and 'Reservoirs'.

'R.S. Thomas is one of the half-dozen best poets now writing in English. He often moves to tears, and certain lines of his impress themselves instantly, and perhaps ineradicably, upon the mind. His example reduces most modern verse to footling whimsy'
– KINGSLEY AMIS

'The most resolute religious poet in English this century...opposed to the materialist ethic of our present age, he remains a mystical, uncompromising seeker after unpalatable verities'
– BERNARD O'DONOGHUE, *Times Literary Supplement*

'His poetry is deeply coloured by his experience of working in remote rural communities, where some of the churches had tiny congregations and where life was harsh and the landscape bleak; he has created his own form of bleak Welsh pastoral, streaked with indignation over the history of Wales and the Welsh'
– MARGARET DRABBLE, *Oxford Companion to English Literature*

'He ranks with the greatest poets of the century and has been called the major one now writing in English. His stature is that of Yeats and Eliot' – *Western Mail*

ISBN 0 906427 96 7   £7.95

Counterpoint
BY
R.S. THOMAS

POETRY BOOK SOCIETY RECOMMENDATION

Counterpoint (1990) shows Thomas again breaking new ground. The themes are familiar, but are given a pointed, contemporary significance: the challenge of scientific knowledge, the threat to the environment, language and the machine age, a mirrored self-consciousness over the act of writing and the stuff of language, and more traditionally, love and waiting and stillness.

Counterpoint is a visionary work, questioning the givenness of God against a suffering world. The bleak Welsh landscape of his earlier work has become a battleground for the questing spirit and the questioning mind. As his poems have grown more austere, more pared down to essentials, Thomas has built them into different shaped collections. Yet the setting of *Counterpoint* is quite unexpected: it is the biblical structure of reality...B.C...Incarnation... Crucifixion... A.D.

The melody of the familiar biblical tune is pitched against the melody of the unfamiliar highly personal interpretation, from the burning bush of Exodus to the 'bush of the imagination we have set on fire'. The resulting counterpoint is a scintillating challenge to the religious mind, and – because it is R.S. Thomas – kindling to the dry, contemporary soul.

'Thomas balances a ton of bleakness against the merest touch of the luminosity of a shadow...a poet-priest who has been looking the difficulties of faith harder and harder in the face...theological poems describing a metaphysical descent without banisters' – DAVID SCOTT, *Church Times*

Paperback: ISBN 1 85224 117 9   £6.95

Mass for Hard Times

BY

R.S. THOMAS

POETRY BOOK SOCIETY RECOMMENDATION

R.S. Thomas has always posed difficult questions in his poems and forced readers to confront uncertainities, ambiguities and the equivocal and paradoxical nature of our experience of life.

In *Mass for Hard Times*, he has drawn together a collection which encompasses all his major areas of questioning. Here are poems about time and history, about the self, about language and the writing of poetry, about love, the machine, the Cross and prayer. In many of the poems clusters of these concerns are movingly and unforgettably imaged in both familiar and new ways: the sea and ships, journeys and travellers, painting, mirrors, science and geological time are intertwined as he questions and reflects.

What is most powerful and original here is the humour and irony of his voice, and his use of some of the classic structures of modern consciousness – the form of the Mass and liturgy, children's rhymes, the seasons and the sonata.

'He has penetrated deeply into the relationship between God and Man in a world dominated by science and materialism. Much of this book is metaphysical poetry in the vein of Donne and Hopkins. It is equally at home with Kant, quantum theory and the computer, displaying an intense intellectual rigour in dazzling images' – DENIS HEALEY, *Sunday Telegraph* (Books of the Year)

Paperback: ISBN 1 85224 229 9   £7.95